Earth
Partners
Saving the Planet

Library of Congress Cataloging-in-Publication Data

Morrison, Yvonne.
   Earth partners : saving the planet / by Yvonne Morrison.
      p. cm. -- (Shockwave)
   Includes index.
   ISBN-10: 0-531-17753-X (lib. bdg.)
   ISBN-13: 978-0-531-17753-2 (lib. bdg.)
   ISBN-10: 0-531-15489-0 (pbk.)
   ISBN-13: 978-0-531-15489-2 (pbk.)
1. Nature--Effect of human beings on--Juvenile literature.
2. Environmental degradation--Prevention--Juvenile literature.
3. Pollution--Prevention--Juvenile literature. I. Title. II. Series.

   GF75.M68 2008
   333.72--dc22

2007016313

Published in 2008 by Children's Press, an imprint of Scholastic Inc.,
557 Broadway, New York, New York 10012
www.scholastic.com

SCHOLASTIC, CHILDREN'S PRESS, and associated logos are trademarks
and/or registered trademarks of Scholastic Inc.

08 09 10 11 12 13 14 15 16 17
10 9 8 7 6 5 4 3 2 1

Printed in China through Colorcraft Ltd., Hong Kong

Author: Yvonne Morrison
Educational Consultant: Ian Morrison
Editors: Nadja Embacher and Nerida Frost
Designer: Steve Clarke
Photo Researcher: Jamshed Mistry

Photographs by: Getty Images (cover; Earth Summit mural, pp. 12–13; Inuit and dogs, p. 17; p. 18;
Chernobyl victim, p. 21; toxic waste, p. 23; p. 26; diver, p. 27; whaling ship, p. 29: GM crops,
pp. 32–33); **©Greenpeace** (p.30); **Jennifer and Brian Lupton** (teenagers, pp. 32–33); **Photolibrary**
(p. 7; p. 15; hippo, p. 27; p. 28; high school students protesting, p. 31; **Stock Central** (p. 3);
Tranz: Corbis (pp. 8–9; United Nations meeting, p. 11; pp. 19–20; anti-nuclear protest, p. 21;
recycling electronics, p. 23; pp. 24–25; chimpanzees with caregiver, p. 29; Japanese
demonstration, p. 31); Reuters (UN peacekeeping, p. 11); Zuma Press (polar bear, p. 17)

Every effort has been made to trace and acknowledge copyright. Where this attempt has proved
unsuccessful, the publisher would be pleased to hear from the photographer or party concerned
to rectify any omissions.

All illustrations and other photographs © Weldon Owen Education Inc.

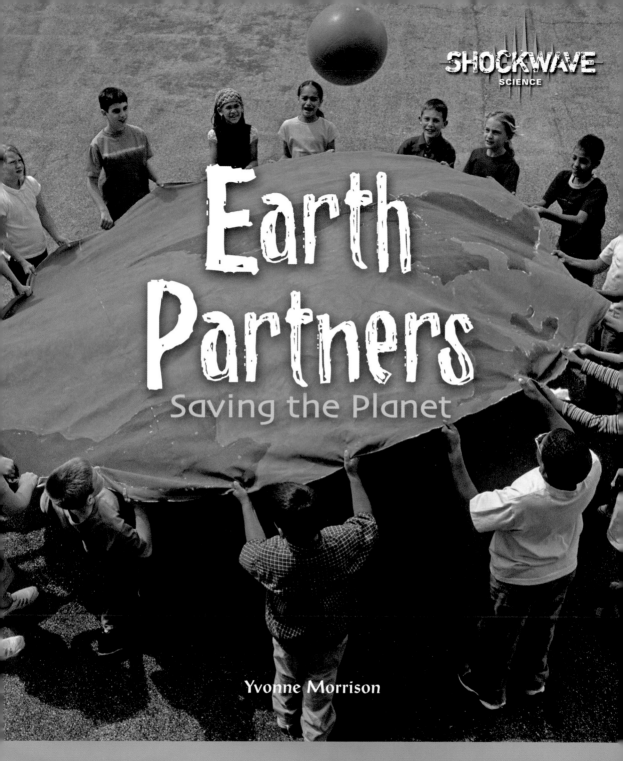

Earth
Partners
Saving the Planet

Yvonne Morrison

children's press®

An imprint of Scholastic Inc.
NEW YORK • TORONTO • LONDON • AUCKLAND • SYDNEY
MEXICO CITY • NEW DELHI • HONG KONG
DANBURY, CONNECTICUT

CHECK THESE OUT!

SHOCKER
Stuff to Shock, Surprise, and Amaze You

Quick Recaps and Notable Notes

Word Stunners and Other Oddities

The Heads-Up on Expert Reading

Links to More Information

CONTENTS

biodiversity (*bye oh duh VUR suh tee*) the variety of different species living in an area

endangered in danger of becoming one of the last of its kind left on the earth

greenhouse gas any gas in the atmosphere that absorbs heat and warms up the earth. Greenhouse gases occur both naturally and as a result of human activity.

ozone a gas in the atmosphere that blocks dangerous ultraviolet (UV) light from reaching the earth's surface

treaty a formal agreement between two or more countries

United Nations an international organization of countries that promotes world peace and human dignity

. . . .

For additional vocabulary, see Glossary on page 34.

Ozone comes from the Greek word *ozein* meaning "to smell." Ozone has a very strong and distinctive odor.

United Nations headquarters in New York City

We hear news stories every day about environmental problems around the world. Sometimes the problems seem too big to be solved. What can one person do? What can one organization do? Some people think that the earth's environmental problems are so enormous that the actions of one country cannot possibly make any difference. Maybe, their thinking goes, all the nations of the world must cooperate in order to preserve and maintain the well-being of our shared planet.

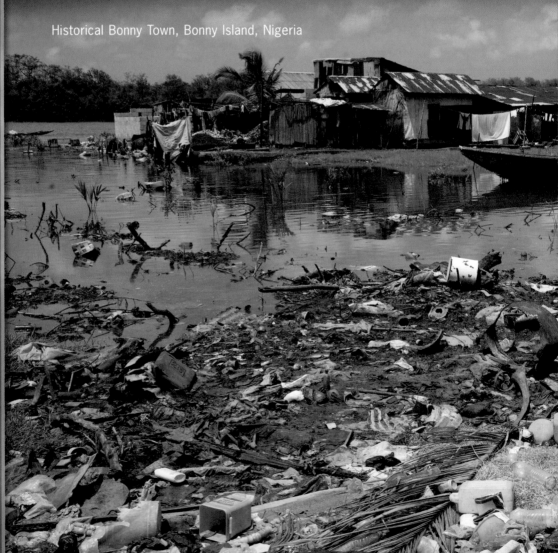

Historical Bonny Town, Bonny Island, Nigeria

More than 50 years ago, countries from around the world took the first steps toward working together to solve global problems. With the increased concerns about the environment, there is more need today than ever before for countries to work together. Protecting the earth is a big job, and we all have to play our part.

Some Global Treaties

International agreements between countries go by different names. Protocols are the least formal.
A **treaty** is more formal. It is a firm legal agreement to do something. In many countries, a treaty is called a convention once it has become law.

- 1945   **United Nations** Charter

  51 countries agree to maintain international peace and security

- 1946   International Convention for the Regulation of Whaling

  42 countries agree to protect whales from overhunting

- 1959   Antarctic Treaty

  12 countries agree to keep Antarctica as a scientific preserve

- 1987   The Montreal Protocol on Substances that Deplete the **Ozone** Layer

  29 countries agree to gradually ban substances that damage the ozone layer

- 1996   Comprehensive Nuclear-Test-Ban Treaty

  71 countries agree not to carry out **nuclear weapons** tests or explosions

Working Together

There are many ways in which countries can cooperate to solve problems. Sometimes nations with common interests form **alliances** to cooperate over a long period of time. Government representatives get together to make agreements. Scientists from different countries come together at international conferences to share information. There are also many organizations around the world run by ordinary people who care deeply about particular issues.

These initiatives all require setting aside political and cultural differences to work for the good of all. The United Nations is the biggest and probably best known of such organizations. The peacekeeping troops of the UN, in their distinctive sky-blue caps or helmets, are familiar figures in areas of conflict around the world.

Organizations large and small, public and private, are making a difference to the future of our planet. They are working in different ways for peace, universal education, and health care. However, none of these efforts will be significant if we destroy the very air we breathe and the land we live on. Protection of the environment is one of the biggest concerns of the twenty-first century.

United Nations Charter

Members agreed to work together on:

- peace and security
- economic and social development
- human rights
- humanitarian affairs
- international law

The heading and opening sentence made me think that this page will feature some of the ways in which people can work together to solve problems. Knowing what to expect makes reading easier, and more fun.

A Spanish UN peacekeeping soldier tries to communicate with children in Lebanon.

The United Nations

After World War II, people were horrified at the extent of human cruelty and destruction that the war had brought. The United Nations was created by 51 countries to work together for peace. Today, the United Nations has 192 member nations.

Agenda 21

In 1992, a United Nations Conference on Environment and Development, called the Earth Summit, was held in Rio de Janeiro, Brazil. **Delegates** from 172 countries came up with a plan for the twenty-first century called Agenda 21. The goal was to ensure that everyone in the world had enough to eat, and that the environment would be kept healthy for future generations. Agenda 21 showed a commitment to change. However, the countries who agreed to it are not required by law to act on it.

Five years after the summit in Rio, a special meeting of the UN found that little progress on Agenda 21 had been made. Environmental damage had continued, and the gap between rich and poor had widened. The costs of putting Agenda 21 into action were estimated at $600 billion. The wealth of many countries relies on industries that contribute to pollution. Finding the balance between economic demands and environmental **sustainability** is not easy. The UN has now set up a special commission to help governments meet the goals of Agenda 21.

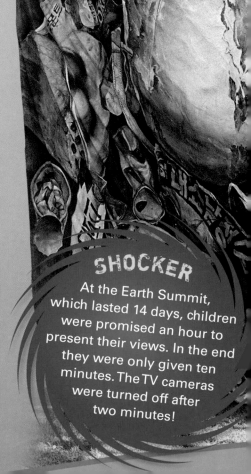

SHOCKER

At the Earth Summit, which lasted 14 days, children were promised an hour to present their views. In the end they were only given ten minutes. The TV cameras were turned off after two minutes!

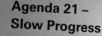

Kids Making a Difference

Twelve-year-old Severn Cullis-Suzuki raised money to attend the Earth Summit. At the event, she gave a speech that earned her a standing ovation. She told delegates:

"At school, even in kindergarten, you teach us to behave in the world. You teach us not to fight with others, to work things out, to respect others, to clean up our mess, not to hurt other creatures, to share – not be greedy. Then why do you go out and do the things you tell us not to do?"

Agenda 21

The following goals were stated:

- to decrease energy use and develop renewable power sources
- to protect **endangered** species and their habitats
- to ban the dumping of hazardous waste at sea
- to ban methods of fishing that strip the sea, and to set fishing limits
- to help people in developing countries make a living through fair trade
- to label less harmful products with eco-labels, and to make them more affordable
- to check the environmental impact of big building projects and make polluters pay taxes and fines
- to reduce disease and help people live healthier lives
- to reduce the amount of waste we produce
- to cooperate more, and to share technology with developing countries

Agenda 21 – Slow Progress

- not required by law to act
- kids not taken seriously
- costs about $600 billion
- polluting companies generate wealth

This painting was displayed in Rio de Janeiro during the Earth Summit in 1992. It shows the artist's view of the many environmental problems that the summit should address.

Ozone Woes

The earth's **atmosphere** contains a thin layer of ozone gas that blocks harmful **ultraviolet light** from the sun. Ultraviolet light causes sunburn, skin cancer, and other health problems. In the 1970s, scientists discovered that the chlorine in chemicals called CFCs (chlorofluorocarbons) destroys ozone. CFCs were used in aerosol spray cans and refrigerators.

Evidence that CFCs were harming the environment came in 1985. Scientists discovered an area over Antarctica where the ozone layer had thinned dramatically. In 1987, many governments signed an agreement called the Montreal Protocol, to ban CFCs. Companies that wouldn't change their technology to get rid of CFCs were taxed and fined. Since then, the amount of CFCs being released into the atmosphere has gradually decreased. Unfortunately, because of the chlorine left in the air from past CFC usage, the ozone layer has continued to thin. It is not expected to return to normal until 2050. However, the Montreal Protocol was a huge success. It was the first time that the world had cooperated on a major environmental problem.

The Growth of the Hole in the Ozone Layer

☐ Ozone layer   ☐ Hole

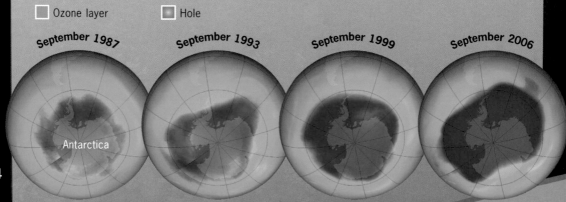

September 1987   September 1993   September 1999   September 2006

Antarctica

Breakdown of the Ozone Layer

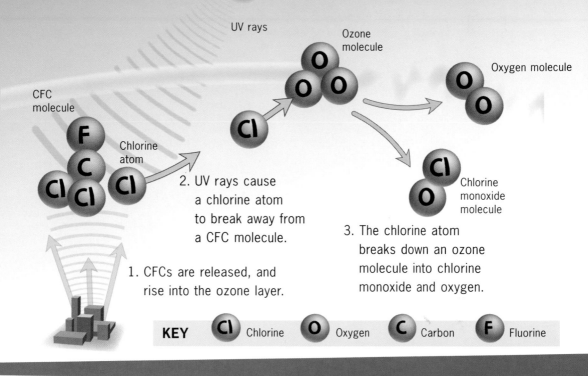

UV rays

Ozone molecule

Oxygen molecule

CFC molecule

Chlorine atom

2. UV rays cause a chlorine atom to break away from a CFC molecule.

1. CFCs are released, and rise into the ozone layer.

Chlorine monoxide molecule

3. The chlorine atom breaks down an ozone molecule into chlorine monoxide and oxygen.

KEY Cl Chlorine   O Oxygen   C Carbon   F Fluorine

Did You Know?

In countries near the ozone hole, such as Australia and New Zealand, people are exposed to far more of the sun's harmful rays than in other parts of the world. People in that part of the world must be especially careful about protecting themselves with sunscreen, hats, and protective clothing.

SHOCKER

In September 2006, the average area of the ozone hole was 10.6 million square miles – bigger than North America!

The light we see (as displayed in a rainbow) ranges from red at one end to violet at the other. *Ultraviolet* means "beyond violet," and is invisible light. *Infrared*, meaning "below red," at the other end of the spectrum, is also invisible.

The Kyoto Treaty

Earth's atmosphere is made up of many gases. Some of these gases, such as **carbon dioxide** and **methane**, are called **greenhouse gases**. They absorb heat and then radiate their heat to the earth, keeping it warm. In the right amounts, this keeps the planet warm enough to support life. However, the earth is getting warmer because of an increase in greenhouse gases. This process is called **global warming**. Some human activities, such as burning fossil fuels, are increasing the amount of greenhouse gases in the atmosphere. Many scientists say this could cause the earth to warm too much. It could lead to modified weather patterns and melting of the polar ice caps.

Scientists around the world agree that steps need to be taken to reduce the amount of greenhouse gases we put in the atmosphere. In 1997, in Kyoto, Japan, people from different countries got together to discuss an agreement called the Kyoto Protocol. This agreement set clear goals for reducing **emissions** within a set time frame. In 2005, the Kyoto Protocol became a legally binding treaty. Now more than 160 countries are involved.

The Greenhouse Effect

Space

Some of the sun's rays are reflected back out to space.

Earth's atmosphere

Greenhouses gases absorb heat from the earth and radiate it out to warm the atmosphere.

16

The traditional lifestyle of the Inuit in Alaska, northern Canada, Russia, and Greenland is threatened by global warming. Hunting is becoming increasingly dangerous in areas where the ice is thinning.

Did You Know?

Hydrofluorocarbons (HFCs) are one of the greenhouse gases the world is trying to reduce. Unfortunately, HFCs have been used to replace CFCs, which were destroying the ozone layer!

The shrinking northern ice cap is forcing Arctic animals to move farther north in search of solid ice.

Kyoto: Too Little, Too Late?

There are different reactions to the Kyoto Treaty around the world. Many scientists feel that the reductions in greenhouse gases required by the treaty are nowhere near great enough to have the desired effect. Yet, even the small reduction in greenhouse gases agreed to by many countries was opposed by many big businesses. Some hired their own scientists to say that greenhouse gases did not affect the planet.

Although the gains of the Kyoto Treaty were not big, many people see them as an important first step. Surprisingly, some of the main supporters of reducing greenhouse gases are big insurance companies. They are having to pay out more and more each year for damage caused by wild weather. They have been forced to acknowledge that the climate is changing.

Many scientists believe that glaciers all over the world are receding due to global warming. This marker was placed in 1978 to show how far the Exit Glacier in Alaska extended at that time. It has receded 1,000 feet in just the last 10 years.

1978

Total Greenhouse-Gas Emissions

1990
2004

8,000
7,000
6,000
5,000
4,000
3,000
2,000
1,000
0

Million tons

United States
Russia
Japan
Germany
Canada
United Kingdom
Italy
France
Australia

Worldwide emissions have decreased by 3.3 percent since 1990. U.S. emissions increased by 15 percent between 1990 and 2004.

The tiny island nation of Tuvalu in the South Pacific is only 15 feet above sea level. As ocean levels rise, Tuvalu is drowning. Some scientists fear it will be the first country to disappear as a result of climate change.

When the author writes "Tuvalu is drowning," I don't think she means it is really drowning! It is just a way of making a strong point. It definitely grabbed my attention.

Ban the Bomb!

Nuclear weapons are powerful bombs that destroy huge areas and generate deadly **radiation**. At the end of World War II, two bombs were dropped on Japan. The cities of Hiroshima and Nagasaki were completely destroyed. Nuclear bombs have never been used in military conflict since then.

Between 1945 and 1953, more than 50 nuclear bombs were exploded for the purposes of testing only. Radiation from these tests made people sick. Campaigns to "ban the bomb" sprang up around the world. In 1963, more than 100 countries signed the Partial-Test-Ban Treaty. It banned nuclear testing in the atmosphere, in space, and underwater, but not underground.

Some of the countries that didn't sign continued to do tests above ground. Many countries that did sign still tested weapons underground. Then, in 1996, a new treaty was signed by 71 countries, that agreed to ban all nuclear weapons testing. The treaty has yet to be **ratified** by many nations, including the United States. Unfortunately, some countries never signed at all.

SHOCKER

There are more than 20,000 nuclear warheads in the world – enough to destroy all the life on earth many times over.

In 1998, these people demonstrated against the testing of nuclear weapons in India.

Did You Know?

Radiation is invisible, odorless, and tasteless. However, exposure to harmful radiation can have terrible effects on health or can even kill. Radiation causes cancer and other serious diseases. It affects not only those exposed directly to it, but also their future children.

In 1986, there was an accident at the Chernobyl Nuclear Power Plant on the border of Ukraine and Belarus in eastern Europe. Harmful radiation affected up to five million people. Since then, there has been a far higher incidence of cancer in the region, particularly in children.

My Waste, Your Problem

Pollution comes from many sources. Nuclear power stations produce radioactive waste. Many factories, such as those that make carpet, paper, or **pharmaceutical** products, produce chemical wastes. What is done with all this waste? Unfortunately, much of it ends up in developing countries. For years, developed nations have dealt with their **toxic** and **radioactive** waste by exporting it. Wealthier countries often pay less wealthy ones to take their waste. Often these countries don't have enough resources to deal with toxic waste safely.

The trade of many kinds of toxic waste is now banned by the Basel Convention. This global agreement on hazardous wastes came into force in 1992. The convention aims to protect human health and the environment. Three of the 170 parties that signed the convention, including the United States, have not yet ratified it. Unfortunately, the Basel Convention does not cover nuclear waste. There is currently no global agreement on trade in nuclear waste.

bans trade in toxic waste

came into effect in 1992

170 parties signed

Basel Convention

3 parties did not ratify

aims to protect human health

aims to protect the environment

SHOCKER

Each year, more than 100 million tons of toxic waste are produced worldwide. About 10 percent of it is exported. No one knows how much is disposed of illegally.

In 1998, 3,000 tons of toxic waste from Taiwan were illegally dumped in Cambodia. After at least one person died and others became ill, protests by local people forced Taiwan to take back the waste.

Old electronics often end up in countries such as China and India. There they are taken apart and recycled. Some parts of this high-tech waste are highly toxic.

The World's Last Wilderness

At the southern end of the world lies a vast, icy continent, surrounded by stormy seas, floating ice, and freezing winds. Antarctica was first explored in 1901. By 1950, several countries were beginning to argue about who owned various part of the continent. Then, in 1957, 12 countries set aside their differences and cooperated in the name of an international year of polar research. The success of that year led to the signing of the Antarctic Treaty, which took effect in 1961.

The Antarctic Treaty has been signed by 46 countries. Every year, the member countries hold meetings and make new rules to protect Antarctica. Despite the treaty, Antarctica faces many threats. Global warming is causing ice shelves to melt and break apart. Tourists leave trash and generate pollution. Waste products take a long time to break down in the cold environment. Overfishing and whaling in the Southern Ocean are also problems.

Scientists monitor the numbers of Adélie penguins in Antarctica. These penguins feed on krill, which are a very important species in the Antarctic food web. Low numbers of penguins indicate a low number of krill in the ocean.

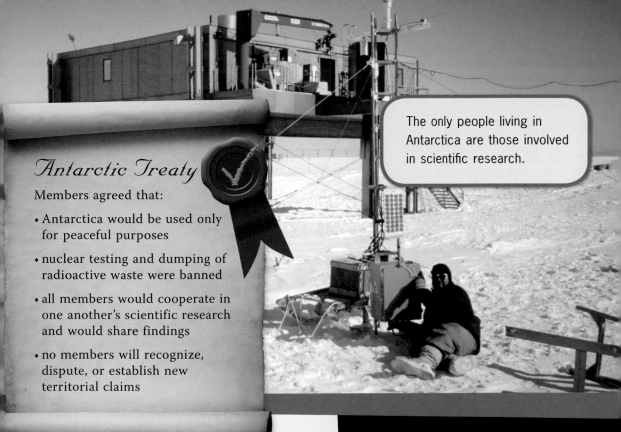

The only people living in Antarctica are those involved in scientific research.

Antarctic Treaty

Members agreed that:

- Antarctica would be used only for peaceful purposes

- nuclear testing and dumping of radioactive waste were banned

- all members would cooperate in one another's scientific research and would share findings

- no members will recognize, dispute, or establish new territorial claims

Territorial Claims in Antarctica

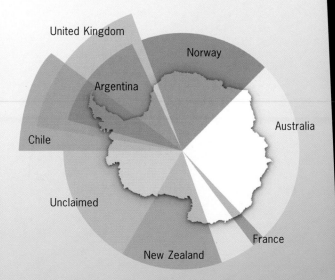

United Kingdom

Norway

Argentina

Chile

Australia

Unclaimed

France

New Zealand

Did You Know?

Seven countries have made claims on parts of Antarctica. These claims are based on discovery and occupation. Only some countries recognize these claims. However, as long as the Antarctic Treaty is in force, nothing can add to or diminish these claims. No country can own Antarctica. All people there are governed by the laws of their own countries.

Species at Risk!

Protecting Our Biodiversity

Animals and plants are vital for the survival of humans. We rely on them for oxygen, food, clothing, shelter, and medicines. Scientists think that there may be as many as ten million species of animals and plants in the world, though only about 1.5 million species have been discovered so far. This **biodiversity** is essential for a healthy environment.

Species are becoming extinct now at a faster rate than at any other time in human history. Human activity is having a negative impact on our natural world. The growing human population needs increasing amounts of land on which to live and grow food. Humans are using up resources, and are creating large amounts of pollution. Around the world, people are clearing rain forests to make room for settlements and farmland.

One square mile of forest is cut down every six minutes. At this rate, all tropical forests will be destroyed by 2040. As habitats are destroyed, species die with them.

A single rain-forest tree can provide a home for 2,000 different species of animal, such as this tiger-striped leaf frog.

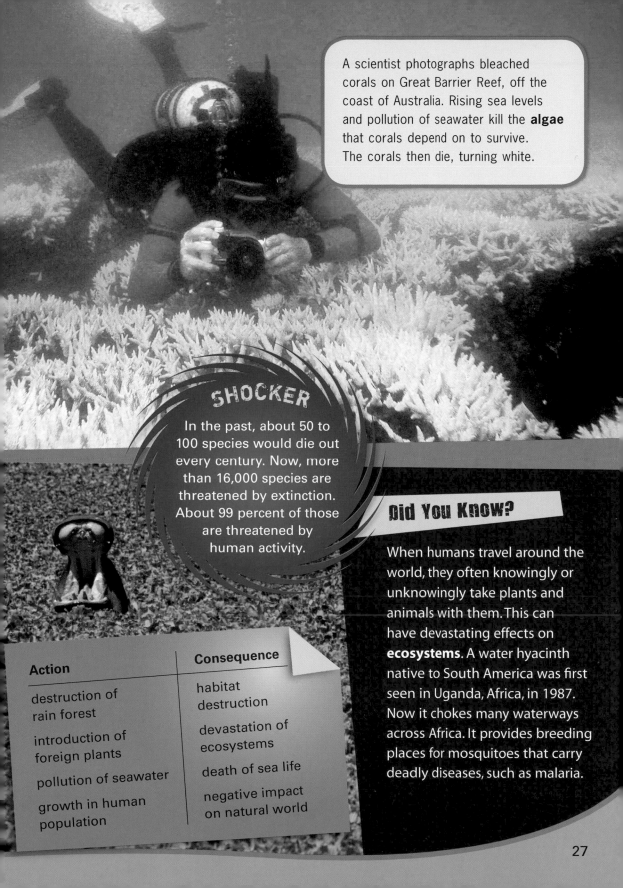

A scientist photographs bleached corals on Great Barrier Reef, off the coast of Australia. Rising sea levels and pollution of seawater kill the **algae** that corals depend on to survive. The corals then die, turning white.

SHOCKER

In the past, about 50 to 100 species would die out every century. Now, more than 16,000 species are threatened by extinction. About 99 percent of those are threatened by human activity.

Did You Know?

When humans travel around the world, they often knowingly or unknowingly take plants and animals with them. This can have devastating effects on **ecosystems**. A water hyacinth native to South America was first seen in Uganda, Africa, in 1987. Now it chokes many waterways across Africa. It provides breeding places for mosquitoes that carry deadly diseases, such as malaria.

Action	Consequence
destruction of rain forest	habitat destruction
introduction of foreign plants	devastation of ecosystems
pollution of seawater	death of sea life
growth in human population	negative impact on natural world

Trading in Endangered Species

International cooperation is needed to protect the world's biodiversity. One very important international agreement is the Convention on International Trade in Endangered Species (CITES). It was drawn up in 1973, and more than 160 countries have signed it. CITES bans or limits trade in thousands of rare plant and animal species and products. Despite these bans, trade continues illegally. Products from endangered species are so valuable that criminals think breaking laws is worth the risk. Poachers around the world hunt many animals supposedly protected by CITES. These species will not be safe until people stop buying products made from the fur of big cats, from tortoise and turtle shells, and from ivory from elephant tusks, for example.

Another important agreement for the protection of biodiversity was reached in 1992, during the Earth Summit in Brazil. The Convention on Biological Diversity has been signed by more than 180 countries. The agreement says that biodiversity on earth is important for human health and well-being.

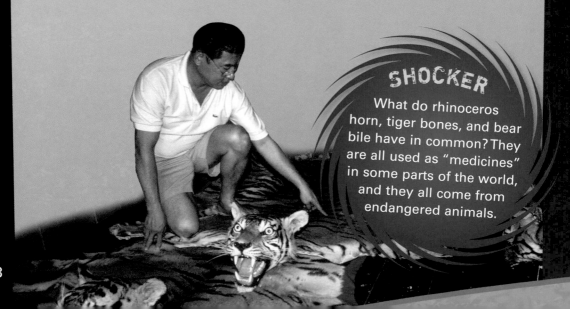

SHOCKER

What do rhinoceros horn, tiger bones, and bear bile have in common? They are all used as "medicines" in some parts of the world, and they all come from endangered animals.

Did You Know?

In 1982, the International Whaling Commission imposed a **moratorium** on commercial whaling. However, some whaling for scientific purposes was still permitted. Japan has used this clause to hunt hundreds of whales each year, including some endangered species. The whale meat from these scientific whaling expeditions is later sold as food.

A Japanese ship pulls an injured whale onboard, as part of a scientific program.

These orphaned chimpanzees were rescued from poachers who planned to sell them as pets. At this sanctuary in Uganda, they are safe and cared for in a natural habitat.

Protecting Our Future

International cooperation is increasingly important. The list of problems the world community needs to solve is getting longer. Peace, world hunger, poverty, education, human rights, and global warming are several of the many issues to be tackled. Governments need to find solutions for these problems on local and international levels.

In the year 2000, the largest gathering of world leaders in history set out a concrete plan of action to address all these issues. The United Nations Millennium Declaration set definite goals to be met by the year 2015. By 2007, the UN announced that progress had been made in many areas. But much remains to be done. Solving all the world's problems will not happen overnight. However, each of us can help to make things happen. We can get informed, get active, and get involved. Protecting the environment, or the world, starts at home.

These teens are taking part in a project to install solar panels.

The United Nations Millennium Declaration:

Some of the goals set out were:

- to rid the world of poverty and hunger
- to ensure that everyone gets an education
- to ensure that men and women are treated equally
- to combat HIV/AIDS, malaria, and other diseases
- to protect the environment globally
- to establish a global partnership for development
- to protect human rights
- to help those who can't help themselves
- to avoid war and conflict

These high-school students are demonstrating against the disappearance of ecosystems.

It can be confusing knowing when to use *ensure*, *assure*, or *insure*. In general:

assure – to promise something

ensure – to take steps to make something happen

insure – to take precautions against the occurrence of something

These young people in Japan are demonstrating for the protection of the environment.

Genetic modification of a plant species means changing its **DNA**, usually to make the plant easier to grow or more nutritious. GM cotton is protected against insects, so that farmers don't need to use as many pesticides. GM golden rice has additional vitamin A, to prevent some diseases. Some people believe that GM crops will produce more food and help solve the world's hunger problem.

WHAT DO YOU THINK?

Do you think that genetically modifying food crops is a good idea?

PRO

It should be up to the people who need the food to decide whether or not to use GM crops. GM crops could actually be good for the environment. People could grow GM crops that don't need to be sprayed with pesticides or don't need as much water.

Scientists testing GM crops

However, many people worry that too little is known about the long-term effects of GM crops. There is debate about unintended effects on the food chain. Insect-resistant GM crops may lead to a decline in some bird species that eat insects, for example. Some consumers want all GM foods labeled, so that they can make informed choices. However, they also worry that GM crops could spread into other crops without people's knowledge.

CON

How do we know if GM crops are safe? If the crops get out of control or don't work as intended they could do more harm than good. A safer solution for world hunger would be a fairer distribution of food supplies.

GLOSSARY

algae (*AL jee*) small plantlike living things without proper roots or stems, that grow in water or damp places

alliance (*uh LYE uhnss*) an agreement or association formed for mutual benefit

atmosphere (*AT muhss feer*) a mixture of gases surrounding a planet

carbon dioxide a gas that plants use to make food, and that plants and animals release into the air when respiring, or breathing

delegate (*DEL uh guht*) a person sent to represent others

DNA the molecules in every cell of an organism that carry the genetic code, which determines characteristics of that organism

DNA

ecosystem (*EE koh siss tuhm*) a community of animals and plants interacting with their environment

emission (*ee MISH uhn*) a substance released into the atmosphere

genetic modification any alteration of genetic material to produce changes in an organism that will be passed along to succeeding generations of that organism

global warming a gradual rise in the temperature of the earth's atmosphere

methane a colorless, odorless gas that is used for fuel

moratorium (*mohr uh TOR ee uhm*) a legal waiting period set by an authority

nuclear weapon an explosive of mass destruction that uses the energy released by splitting atoms

pharmaceutical (*far muh SU ti kuhl*) referring to the developing, producing, and selling of medicines

radiation energy released from nuclear explosions, causing sickness and death

radioactive giving off harmful radiation

ratify to approve officially

sustainability (*suh stain uh BIL i tee*) the ability to be continued without long-term negative impact on the environment

toxic (*TOK sik*) poisonous

ultraviolet light energy rays with a shorter wavelength than visible light

FIND OUT MORE

BOOKS

Apte, Sunita. *Polar Regions: Surviving in Antarctica*. Bearport Publishing, 2005.

Burnie, David. *Endangered Planet*. Kingfisher, 2004.

Metcalf, Gene and Metcalf, Tom. *Nuclear Power*. Greenhaven Press, 2006.

Redlin, Janice L. *Saving the Natural World*. Weigl Publishers, 2006.

Ross, Stewart. *United Nations*. Raintree, 2003.

Tarsitano, Frank. *United Nations*. World Almanac Library, 2003.

WEB SITES

Go to the Web sites below to learn more about global warming and endangered species.

www.epa.gov/climatechange/kids

www.worldwildlife.org/endangered

www.ace.mmu.ac.uk/kids/globalwarming.html

www.dnr.state.wi.us/org/caer/ce/eek/earth/air/global.htm

http://tiki.oneworld.net/global_warming/climate1.html

INDEX

ABOUT THE AUTHOR

Yvonne Morrison has traveled to more than twenty countries. She believes all of the treaties in this book show that the countries of the world can cooperate. Yvonne says that the Antarctic treaty is a wonderful idea, and she would love to visit the unspoiled wilderness of Antarctica one day. Yvonne lives with her husband in an old-fashioned cottage in a sunny seaside town in New Zealand. Her hobbies are dancing, listening to music, collecting antiques, and reading.